NLP

Using Subliminal Manipulation And Secret Techniques To Overcome Deception, Brainwashing, And Covert Nlp, You Can Influence And Win People

(An Effective Approach To Cultivate Personal Growth)

Nikola Firsov

TABLE OF CONTENT

Case Studies Of Dark Psychology 1

Adjectives And Adverbs Of Commentary 17

Avoid Words And Use Body Language 30

How Can NLPHelp You Influence Others? What Is Nlp? 40

The Benefits Of Priming As A Technique 51

What Does A Psychologist Understand By Psychopathy? 66

Nlp-Based Mind Control For Love And Relationships 89

Several Instances Of Manipulation In Our Everyday Lives 97

Self-Mastery 112

The Basics Of Nonverbal Communication 119

Case Studies Of Dark Psychology

This handbook has taken the time to discuss the various facets of dark psychology, which is an effective instrument in the hands of a manipulator. It's time to examine a few case studies, or illustrations, of how They applied these various real-world techniques. Recall that the case studies in this chapter provide severe illustrations of dark psychology across human history, illuminating its mechanisms.

Ted Bundy's Last Testament

Possibly the most well-known serial killer in history is Ted Bundy. The quantity of information that has been released about him, the crimes he committed, and how eager Bundy was to participate in interviews are some of the most intriguing aspects of his tale. The fascination and intensity of hoopla surrounding many other high-profile offenders frequently surpass the actual crime committed.

But with Bundy, this is most definitely not the case. The overall number of confirmed homicides connected to Ted Bundy is still unknown. Although he was only charged with 30, he has indicated that the true number is likely closer to 100. Nobody is certain, and many analysts believe that Bundy is even unaware of the number of individuals he murdered.

Numerous facts regarding Bundy's atrocities have contributed to our understanding of the world of psychotic serial killers, their tactics, and some of their motivations. Bundy was aware of the influence public view and perception can have. Unquestionably, he was handsome and pleasant to many of the persons he encountered, even during the commission of these killings.

This is a defining characteristic of psychopaths, who can project an attractive and charming exterior without having any interior reality to match. When you pause to contemplate that a human being was able to arouse affection and comfort in his victim's final minutes before killing them in some of the greatest crimes in history, you can see how emotionally detached and cold-blooded men like Ted Bundy were.

Hitler

There are a lot of political similarities between Adolf Hitler's political career and some of Machiavelli's theories. It is often the case that Hitler is the clearest example of what a contemporary Machiavellian leader will resemble. Hitler and Niccol Machiavelli believed peace should be merely a temporary respite from an endless battle. Hitler strongly desired to conquer and intended to utilize the Third Reich. Hitler was a perfect example of a warrior ruler who never stopped.

To achieve a preconceived political goal, Machiavelli also supported the creation of reality and its subsequent modification. Hitler's notorious fundamental philosophy called for the persecution and eradication of the majority of the German Jewish population. The Reichstag Fire, a false flag operation, is the primary incident that facilitated Hitler's work on this.

Machiavelli's political philosophy also includes the fundamental notion that power is a noble objective in and of itself. Whatever strategies a person uses to seize and maintain power might be supported by the behavior expected of a leader.

Hitler is a great illustration of this idea in action. Hitler was a master at playing on the nation's emotions and thoughts while simultaneously influencing the governmental structure that was in place.

Examining textbooks makes it simple to observe the adoration, awe, and love that Hitler was able to arouse in the German people during that period.

Yes, we have now depicted Hitler as the embodiment of evil, but at the time, he was skilled at inciting both fear and affection in his subjects. Take a peek at some of the Hitler speech recordings to witness this.

Rasputin: Magic or Dark Psychology?

Examining case studies on dark psychology would be incomplete without considering Rasputin and all that this monk has stood for. Rasputin's authority in this area has reverberated far into the future, making him an intriguing character. It even influenced many later-emerging charismatic influencers in some way. Rasputin was a spiritual leader who could sway the ruling Russian dynasty. Rasputin found him attractive because of his ability to portray an alluring blend of sensuality and religiosity that could be projected onto nearly any aspect of a person.

The monk's apparent healing abilities greatly impressed others who might have been more inclined to join the religion.

However, individuals who delighted in the world's physical pleasures may also find merit in Rasputin's persona. The most significant aspect of Rasputin's persona was his dual nature as an angel and a devil.

Many facets of Rasputin's hypnotically-induced effect can still be seen in modern times. One of the most notorious—and maybe the first—people to put his victims in a state akin to a trance or suggestibility was Grigori Rasputin. What were these purportedly Rasputin's healing and hypnotic abilities?

It is thought that he was able to instill in his victims a profound sense of peace, tranquility, and relaxation. He is renowned for his capacity to reduce any aches and pains that members of the Russian family were experiencing at the time. This enhanced his appeal and made him more influential to everyone around him.

Also, Rasputin engaged in several actions now typical of covert emotional manipulation. The fact that Rasputin never gave the impression of attempting to exert control over his victims is one of the reasons he had such a profound effect on the people around him. Alternatively, he would appear as someone with an enigmatic ability to which people would submit. These are all characteristics of contemporary covert emotional manipulation.

For individuals who want to learn more about charismatic influence, the case study of Rasputin is pertinent. Similar to Rasputin, many contemporary dark psychological manipulators can draw followers due to the belief that they have hidden or unique knowledge.

In Rasputin's day, this idea was far more practical. Rational and scientific thought were less advanced, and the world was not accustomed to this kind of deception as it is now. This lends additional support to the notion that.

Rasputin was a strong, holy individual. Dark psychology scholars will find many similarities between the persuasiveness of a supernatural portrayal and similarly compelling contemporary leaders who pretend to be spiritual to acquire the power and influence they desire. Rasputin's biography demonstrates the connection between psychological power and sexual expressiveness.

Rasputin used his sinister influence to lead a life of extravagant extravagance and even promiscuity, just like many people have done throughout history. It is no accident that cult leaders, wherever they may be found or how they choose to practice, are frequently observed taking pleasure in the members they select. Although Rasputin is a well-known example, he is not the original user of these methods.

Which Meta-programs are commonly used?

The main goal is to increase sales and maintain enduring client relationships to increase productivity. Selecting the appropriate NLPpattern requires a thorough examination of meta-programs. Recognize that they are a solution to assist the consumer in developing stronger, more knowledgeable decision-making abilities and a collection of guidelines offering a definition of behavior. Below is an explanation of some of the most frequently seen meta-programs that are based on human characteristics and inclinations:

Towards / Away From: People with a "towards" attitude are typically upbeat, proactive, and driven to finish activities to feel a sense of accomplishment. Sellers can use this to instill a desire in them for the good or service they are willing to provide since they respond best to strategies that involve bargaining or motivation. On the other hand, the opposing conduct is defined by the 'away from' feature. These folks often steer clear of trouble and pay little attention to it. They are, therefore, more uncertain and pessimistic about their choice. Since they will likely look for rapid solutions to defuse tension, pressure-based persuasion techniques will be effective since they will cause them to behave impulsively.

Internal / External: The primary distinction between personality qualities that are internal and external is the origin of inspiration. Some consumers base their future decisions on internal elements, such as their past experiences, and they will only consider other people's comments in conjunction with their ideas and beliefs. This is a challenge for sellers, but it may be overcome by taking a more emotional, human approach that mirrors the buyer's to help him see the worth of the goods. On the other hand, those who rely on outside influence are more objective and susceptible to persuasion. Acquiring information regarding user reviews, customer comments, and product ratings can enable the merchant to persuade potential customers.

Procedures / Options: Those who fall into the "options" category are open-minded and imaginative individuals who want to have a choice in anything presented. The sellers are responsible for offering chances that give them a spread to consider. Consequently, individuals tend to choose newer items they haven't tried before and react well to creative ways of presenting concepts and tactics, such as trials and presentations. On the other hand, those who are more "procedures" oriented are more inflexible and value structure over flexibility. A seller must adopt frameworks and defined parameters connected to the product to be allowed to sell to these individuals.

Same / Different: The buyer's response to change differs between these two characteristics. Individuals who adopt the "same" mindset oppose or resist goods and services that require changing their lives. They are not active decision-makers and need the seller to reassure them that everything is normal. Customers are more open to accepting differences and are easier to sell since they enjoy change. Presenting all the ways the product can improve their lives can persuade them.

Reactive vs. Proactive: Proactive individuals take swift action when they are satisfied. They are action-takers who possess the ability to make snap decisions. Sellers may approach them and present compelling details about their goods or services. Reactive individuals frequently make decisions more slowly than others and consider both sides of an issue before deciding. They either remain silent while assessing situations or examine any circumstance that has a chance of going wrong. The vendor must exhibit patience and a strong sense of conviction to the buyer.

General / Specific: Some people find generalized knowledge and a broader perspective appealing. Because people prefer a quick comprehension to a detailed review, product overviews can assist customers in making better judgments and provide them with a more comprehensive viewpoint. It takes a little longer to persuade people with certain tastes since they won't buy a good or service unless they know the "specific" details. This kind of buyer requires thorough information and explanations before being prepared to purchase. Thus, sellers must be able to answer their inquiries.

Thinkers / Feelers: Thinkers are intellectual beings who use logical reasoning. Their propensity to evaluate goods and services before becoming completely sold on them is what makes them unique. Sellers must possess sufficient knowledge to furnish details and elucidate their claims. On the other hand, feelers relate their choices to feelings and are influenced by creative and spontaneous approaches. Sentiment and descriptive techniques that can help the buyer "feel" as though he needs the good or service should be used by the seller.

Pessimistic vs. optimist: Optimistic individuals can think positively even in adverse circumstances. They do better when allowed to weigh the best options. Selling can persuade people by providing examples of how the product can improve their lives. Conversely, pessimists are more receptive to problem-solving strategies. Therefore, vendors must persuade them that their product or service is infallible.

A seller's ability to persuade and negotiate can be enhanced by thoroughly understanding certain personality features. To keep an eye on this process, you must have a sharp sense of observation and well-organized reactions.

Adjectives and Factive Verbs

Factive verbs and adjectives examples are strange, aware, know, realize, and regret.

Active verbs and adjectives emphasize how people learn something, and because they assume the realization is true, they have much power. Let's look at the main structure:

Unusually, X. This sentence presupposes that X is true.

25.) It's odd that people discover so many various uses for my goods.

This example presumes that your product has numerous diverse uses. It also presumes that plenty of people are buying your product, utilizing it, and finding its uses, so it also creates social evidence.

This presumes that people who use the product can accomplish something extremely strong with it—you don't directly explain what, but this helps your reader picture all of your product's great uses. It's incredibly hypnotic since they'll imagine experiencing the benefits after buying it. This also produces social proof—other people think your product is also powerful.

27.) It's hard for many folks not to understand how fantastic this product is.

This sentence is in the negative, yet notice how negation doesn't modify the presupposition of a sentence. This scenario still presumes that many individuals have bought the product, providing social proof. It also presumes that consumers know that your product is fantastic.

28.) You'll only regret that you didn't get it sooner.

This one presumes that you've purchased the product already, and stating a "regret" is a striking contrast from the benefits you've presumably presented about your product.

Again, this is highly mesmerizing because you had to have previously done something to regret something. By regretting not acquiring the product sooner, your audience will have to visualize themselves buying the thing, looking back, and wishing they had bought it sooner.

Adjectives And Adverbs Of Commentary

Commentary Adverbs and Adjectives Examples: thankfully, fortunately, swiftly, swiftly, and anything ending in ly Adverbs and adjectives with commentary have great force since whatever follows them is automatically considered true, even if your audience doesn't agree with what you're saying.

Fortunately, my product is the greatest.

It'd be excellent if they agreed with this! This statement assumes that your product is the greatest available. Even if they don't agree with what you're saying, they will ostensibly agree that your product is the greatest by thinking, "Well, it's not lucky that your product is the best." They are disputing that your product's superiority isn't due to chance.

Fortunately, the discounted rate is valid for a few more days.

This assumes that your product is undervalued, given the value you're providing, and that your price is lower than it usually is to entice customers to buy immediately. Additionally, it subtly conveys a sense of scarcity—as if your product is so in demand that it is restricted, and if they don't buy immediately, they might miss the chance to have it.

A fantastic technique to instill a fear of losing out in your audience is to imply scarcity. This will motivate them to take action.

31.) Luckily, you may still take advantage of the 50% discount many others have already received if you purchase this product now.

This example assumes a significant discount that appears to be about to expire, even if the deal lasts for the next 20 years. Additionally, it requires social proof—many people have benefited from the deal.

32.) Many people quickly realize how helpful this is.

It's wonderful that this example assumes your product is easy to use and takes effect quickly! For this reason, your product needs to be clear and simple to use. Social evidence generated by "many people" also assumes your product is highly beneficial.

33.) My list is getting popular on the internet quite quickly.

This assumes your list is already "hot" and continues getting hotter. Now, the reader is free to interpret what "hot" means. It might indicate that it's growing, providing you with social proof. It could indicate that the value of the information is increasing. They are free to infer what hot means to them, and they will invariably infer something significant.

Typical Numbers

First, second, and third are some examples of ordinal numbers.

Ordinal numbers are particularly hypnotic because, when you employ one, the reader will involuntarily infer that you are enumerating a vast list of items.

34.) As soon as you download this product, you'll see it's completely functional.

This is a mesmerizing way to project the reader into the future by assuming they have already downloaded the product. Using "first" assumes that after downloading the product, they will notice a lot more things and come up with other ideas that will be helpful.

35.) Another free eBook is what you'll get as soon as you join my list.

They will have to assume what the first thing is if you say a "second thing" without mentioning the first. Saying "another" free eBook implies that the recipient has already gotten something for free. This makes the reader imagine a future in which they have already benefited from a free product, are receiving all of this additional value, and will still receive an even greater benefit in the form of a free eBook. That is an extremely strong sentence!

This assumes that your product is useful and has abundant social proof. Using the word "first" suggests that the reader will notice various things when they purchase the goods.

Cleft Phrases

Use of cleft sentences: it is, it was, etc.

Cutting a sentence in half or using a cleft sentence structure allows you to offer several ideas to the reader's subconscious. They'll struggle to argue with you if you say X equals Y. They will have to unconsciously accept the other half of the statement if they disagree with half of it.

The Composition of a Cleft Sentence: The rationale behind (intended belief: the idea you want the reader to believe) is (believable reason).

To better understand cleft sentences, let's look at a few instances.

37.) My fountain pen's crimson color attracts so many people.

Your reader will notice the redness in your goods and conclude, "Oh yeah, that's obviously true," leading them to believe that it must be well-liked, providing social proof. Sort of like a cause-and-effect structure, cleft sentences employ it. When they purchase it, it also serves as self-justification for them; they'll say to themselves, "Oh, I bought it because it was red."

38.) My recent spike in business has persuaded me to temporarily reduce my rates.

This example assumes that your price is already low and will make the reader wonder why you're experiencing a recent consumer rise. Additionally, it indicates scarcity and provides social proof for your product, giving customers the impression that they must move swiftly to take advantage of the reduced costs.

Adverse Thoughts

It is important to realize that most negative thoughts originate from an inner critic, an angry voice in our heads that accuses and berates us as though they were someone else in front of us. Usually, this inner critic serves multiple purposes:

It will criticize you when no one else is around to do it.

It will guilt-trip you into believing you failed to fulfill a duty.

It will ensure you understand that your deficiencies are permanent and that there is little chance of improvement.

The next time something bad happens, pay attention to the words you use to yourself. You'll probably find that it sounds something like this:

"You did a terrible job in the interview. If you go on and on like this, you will never get over this point. You ought to speak more succinctly."

"You failed that exam. You can't possibly pass this class with that kind of work. You ought to put more effort into your studies."

When no one else is around to support us, we construct a second persona in our minds that exists just to punish ourselves. The first indication that it's not worth beating ourselves up over should be that no one is there to do it for us; still, we go above and beyond to fill that hole.

Moreover, observe the implicit finality of these exchanges. There seems to be a subtle but pervasive charge that we will always be this way when we accuse ourselves. We imply that we are lazy and prone to procrastination when we tell ourselves these things, and we always will. It implies that you are timid and terrible at connecting with people, and you always will be when you tell yourself these things.

Lastly, remember that while it may seem like a great way to remind ourselves of our goals, having continual reminders that we should be doing something acts as a weapon for guilt. It serves as a reminder that we are not quite reaching our goals of perfection.

Owning the debate in the first person is necessary to quiet the inner critic and move into content reframing. Instead of using personas or self-accusations to criticize ourselves, we need to discuss "I" and "myself." Eliminating the other person from the equation allows us to be in charge of our opinions without defending those of an unreal third party.

After destroying the inner critic, we need to concentrate on taking the financial implications out of self-accusation. Finality keeps us from thinking we can change and go one step closer to the person we want to be. It's challenging to muster the willpower to address our faults if we are trapped in the notion that they will always exist. Alternatively, we might just kick back and accept that our lives are meant to be mediocre and that our shortcomings are unavoidable. Do you think that's a healthy belief? Most likely not.

How, therefore, can we combat this finality? We take a cue from global business owners, saying "Yes, and..." Yes, and... has magic in its simplicity. Any phrase or concept that ends with it offers up a world of options, and its sole hard-and-fast rule is that we have to figure out what comes next. It expands our horizons and opens up new opportunities.

I'm a bad learner. Indeed, and...

I am aware of my bad study habits. Indeed, and...

That's something I want to alter. Indeed, and...

I need assistance in making that change. Indeed, and...

Alright, I could check up on articles on improving my academic performance, or I could speak with my friend who is doing incredibly well. Indeed, and...

I'm sure that doing that will help me become a better student and enhance my performance. Fantastic!

Just taking away the initial statement's tinge of finality brings this inner dialogue to a new level. Nothing about us that is intangible is genuinely lasting in any aspect of life. We always have the power to change how we act, behave, interact with others, and work toward our objectives. All it takes is the conviction that the screenplay is never complete.

We may refine the message we send ourselves by letting go of our inner critic and substituting a sense of potential for a sense of finality.

We have a terrible word we love to use: "should."

I ought to have been more aware.

That was not the right thing for me to say.

I ought to have worked harder.

Unfortunately, "should" draws attention to our flaws subliminally. It imposes an oppressive sense of accountability on us, accusing us of behaving contrary to some vague expectation of... what? The cosmos? We must use more positive language when reframing, like "can," "could," or "have the ability to," to promote possibilities.

I can study harder the next time because it offers a sense of possibilities for the future without holding us accountable for our past acts. I should have studied harder because it focuses on the past, which we cannot change.

Making sure that any thoughts on our weaknesses are expressed in the past tense is a final tip to consider. Separating a weakness from our current selves gives us more power to alter our thoughts and behaviors. Saying "I have a weakness" can be difficult for some people to accept and get over. There is a conflict between our desired selves and our true selves. However, employing the past tense suggests that we have the freedom to be the individuals we want to be today. We can cultivate the idea that, having grown from our mistakes and chosen a new course for the future, we already embody the qualities of the person we wish to be.

The next time you think of something you want to alter about yourself, try it. Move to the past tense and state, "I have been disorganized in the past, but after seeing the stress it causes, I chose to become a more organized person" instead of "I am terribly disorganized." This change in viewpoint releases a burden from you and creates many opportunities.

Avoid Words And Use Body Language

One language that all people share, to some degree, is body language. Body language, also called non-verbal cues, is the subtle signals our bodies send out about our deepest feelings, intentions, and ideas. Body language manifests in standing, sitting, moving, and making gestures. Even while our voices might indicate, "Oh, I'm so happy!" our bodies can express our actual emotions; perhaps you weren't as joyful as you claimed to be.

Unbeknownst to most of us, nonverbal communication is considerably more significant. When we are young, it is among the earliest forms of communication we encounter. As neonates, we are unable to understand or respond to spoken language. Because they know this, our parents and other caregivers tend to us with affection and regular eye contact, providing us with a language we can comprehend. Adults can also tell how newborns feel by seeing how much they wiggle and smile.

As adults, we also pick far more emotional cues from others than we may think. For instance, on a given day, we might observe that our friend appears to be feeling unfriendly or irritated with you because she spends a significant amount of time with her back to us. When a man leans in close to talk to a lady, it could be interpreted as a sign of sexual attraction. Have you ever found yourself abruptly changing your hairstyle and outfit in front of someone? Whether it's a job interview or an exciting first date, you may have been anxious about making an impression on this individual.

Most of us know the significance of body language and how to take advantage of it on an unconscious and intuitive level. With our shoulders back and heads held high, we could have a little more bounce when we enter a nightclub wearing stylish new attire. We act in a way that communicates our confidence to others because we look nice. Sometimes, when someone else makes a joke, we look at each other, momentarily amused. One of the most common ways humans communicate is through body language.

Without body language, it would be very difficult for us to interpret what people are saying when they speak, and far more difficult to develop an initial opinion of some. Body language can provide crucial information about a person we are speaking with, such as whether they like us, are attracted to us, dislike us, are nervous, or are lying. Words can only tell us where to be or what happened.

Nonverbal Signs Relating to Sitting

As simple as sitting seems, that is precisely what it is. On the other hand, our sitting positions might tell us a lot about who we are. You can learn much about someone's mental and emotional health and true feelings towards you by observing how they sit.

Nearby

Have you ever noticed how near they are to you when enjoying a pleasant cup of coffee on a bench with someone? They appear to have gotten closer since the start of the talk and are leaning in to listen to what you say. You can tell whether someone enjoys your company and wants to feel close to you (romantically or platonically) if they sit close to you. However, sitting a little too far away or pulling away when you approach implies that they don't really enjoy your company or that they don't trust you too much.

Crossed Legs

When they speak, many people cross one leg over the other. Someone is dominant and self-assured when they cross their ankle over their knee and relax on top of it. When someone is at ease and self-assured, they tend to reveal three bodily parts: the crotch, the neck, and the belly button. By exposing these sensitive spots, someone is expressing that they feel comfortable and secure. On the other hand, crossing or locking your legs at the ankles could be a sign of shyness or nervousness. When someone is apprehensive or at an interview, such as meeting their partner's parents, they frequently cross their legs at the ankle.

One knee over the other is the most frequent technique for people to cross their legs, and it can be done either way. Someone is more likely to like you and want to spend time with you if they cross their leg toward you. When someone crosses their leg away from you, it may indicate that they are not interested in you sexually or that they want to put some space between you.

Shaking and tapping the feet

This is a prime illustration of fidgeting. A person shaking their foot or jiggling their leg on the ball of their foot is probably nervous or irritable. This explains why we witness this behavior so frequently in waiting areas and during exams—both settings where expectations are high!

Spread Legs

Spreading their legs while sitting is an attempt at dominance. This posture opens up the bodies and takes up much room. When a man exposes his crotch area to someone in the preferred sex group, it may also be interpreted as a sign of attraction.

Nonverbal Indications Related To The Arms

Yes, the arms, indeed! We use them for dancing, working out, hugging, and waving to people. Because they function as a sort of portal to our torso, a rather susceptible area of our body, the arms are a fascinating method our body can communicate with other people. In light of this, arms can reveal much about a person's emotional state. Thus, it can be helpful to know what to look out for.

With arms crossed

Be ready for a potentially uncomfortable conversation when someone crosses their arms in front of them and folds them in front of their chest. If someone acts this way in response to a question you ask them, they can feel obstinate, agitated, nervous, or insecure. They might also attempt to build a wall between you and the other person to emotionally remove themselves from you. Fear not, though, since this move can also indicate that the person is reflecting carefully on what you have just said or requested, particularly if the rest of their body language appears rather relaxed.

Hands-on the hips, one or both

Standing in this way frequently conveys confidence and power to the point of aggressiveness or hatred. The torso is being blocked by pointed elbows that almost seem to be screaming, "Don't come any closer!" Someone with one or both hands on their hips may attempt to project confidence and independence; otherwise, why do fashion models frequently adopt this stance?

Arms Waving During Speech

Emotionally, this gesture might be interpreted in two ways. Someone may show excitement or annoyance by waving their arms and wringing their hands. The individual exhibiting this behavior is exceedingly agitated or aroused.

Nonverbal Communication Linked to Finger and Hand Motions

We use our hands and fingers for tasks requiring skill and focus. Hands can grasp small objects and point with the fingers to visible objects. Babies learn about their agency through their hands and fingers—just peek at how powerful their little grasp can be!

The Shook Hands

Let's say hello. Most individuals would put out their hands and take solid hold of the other person's, attempting not to be too tight but also not to be too loose that they come across as bashful or distant. A handshake is usually an indication of warmth and friendship from someone. They're eager to talk to you more and want to get to know you.

Grasping the Nose

A liar may occasionally start rubbing their nose in response to an inquiry. Although it could seem random, there are biological facts that support the reason why this occurs. The body releases hormones when someone lies, which causes some blood to rush to the face. Anyone who experiences even a small amount of tingling or itching may find that they are drawn to the parts that feel this way. Not only will the liar be aware of what they are doing, but they won't even notice that they have a slight itchy nose.

Hands Behind the Back

This pose's most noticeable feature is how exposed the body is. Be wary of someone who permits such vulnerability. Giving someone the finger behind the back can be interpreted as a symbol of submission. Conversely, it can also imply confidence because exposing so much of the torso shows that the wearer believes they won't be harmed.

Bringing the Palms to Light

One method to expose oneself is to show off their wrists and hands. Just consider the wrist's numerous tiny veins and the palms' sensitivity. Unexpectedly, exposing these places demonstrates a greater degree of openness and trust. People express openness and reliability when showing you their wrists and palms. Someone subtly tells you they have nothing to hide when they show you their palms.

How Can NLP Help You Influence Others? What Is Nlp?

First things first: you must become familiar with the fundamentals of neuro-linguistic programming if you hope to affect people favorably. An explanation of this idea and how it can benefit both you and other people will be provided in the following paragraphs.

The notion of Neuro-Linguistic Programming, or NLP for short, was created in California by mathematician and linguist Richard Bandler and John Grinder, respectively. In the 1970s, they began to establish this specific notion of therapy.

This might be characterized as the psychotherapy and personality development communication approach.

When conversing with someone else, the individual employing NLP can use specific phrases and gestures to directly impact the other person's behavior. In each given setting, the primary objective of NLPis to elicit alternative reactions and modalities of communication in addition to varied perceptual modifications.

The current relationship could be more intimate or professional. No matter where you are, after connecting with NLP, you will feel in control of your decisions and their positive effects on others.

Professional performance and communication can also be enhanced or improved using this kind of psychological programming.

You can use NLPto alter your reality and ensure you have the self-assurance to confront your fear if you want to improve or gain more confidence when speaking with others.

It is not an easy task to apply NLPto oneself, particularly if you are attempting to transform undesirable behavior and years of trauma. The fact that you can start the healing process is crucial, though.

The following paragraphs will cover the various ways to apply NLPto oneself and others through various strategies that can undoubtedly influence behavior and mind in a much more positive way.

Using Body Language to Gain Understanding of Human Thought and Behavior

Our body's exterior receptors and the daily messages that flow through our nervous system enable us to frequently interpret verbal cues and physical movements.

This improves our ability to interact with others and share our worldview.

One of the finest ways to begin communicating on a much more personal level is to interpret body language.

We can communicate with someone without actually speaking to them by using our interpretations.

We can tell how they will respond to certain things we say before we tell them by observing them.

For instance, it's safe to presume that someone has preconceived notions about you based on what you say if you observe them frowning at something odd you say about yourself. You, in turn, receive back what you say. You can reasonably assume that if you are speaking seriously, they don't agree with what you are attempting to convey.

Another illustration would be a shift in voice tone when someone becomes ecstatic about eating or seeing their favorite celebrity. These modifications will dictate the subject's response to their inputs even without appropriate communication.

These insignificant acts can also provide the spectator with hints regarding the opinions that others may have of them or their speech.

However, developing your ability to read body language is not a simple task. A certain degree of sensitivity to minute variations in human behavior is required. You can tell if someone views you favorably or unfavorably by seeing how they interact with you once you accept these changes.

Gaining an Understanding of Body Language about NLP

Once you can understand body language, you can also decipher minute variations in a person's appearance and body temperature simply by observing them.

By interpreting these shifts, you will converse with them and use language that either worsens their condition or calms them down.

Knowing what to say and how to say it is crucial. The main goal of neuro-linguistic programming is this: manipulating the emotions of others by words and deeds.

Once you can accomplish this, altering people's perspectives of the world will be simple.

In the following paragraphs, we will provide some of the best methods for testing Neuro-Linguistic Programming. So, why do you hesitate? Proceed with this journey without stopping. You won't look back on your choice to act on it straight away.

Individual Recognition

NLPprovides several excellent methods to assist you in cultivating your appreciation, but you must first ascertain your current self. Identifying oneself is a multifaceted task, as most of us have multiple facets of our lives contributing to our identity. In addition to our careers, we also play the parts of parents, friends, and partners.

You are the sum of all your jobs and experiences, yet you are also all of this. You are who you are today because of everything you have from birth, everything you have learned along the way, and everything your life experiences have taught you.

We all share certain characteristics with those connected to us and influential in our formative years. You can have much in common with your mother, father, brother, or sister. However, you are also unique, far more so than you may realize.

Our minds process experiences using a method known as "Meta-Models." Most of the time, these models are beneficial. One such model is the generalization, which prevents us from repeatedly learning the same things (like how to tie your shoes). But drawing too many conclusions at once can be detrimental.

Remove Yourself From Those Negative Feelings

An NLPapproach called dissociation helps people eliminate emotional patterns arising from outside influences. People with performance anxiety or phobias, like a fear of heights, have reported success with this strategy. The method is quite straightforward and absorbable. The idea behind this strategy is to have the subject watch their conduct from a spectator's perspective, which will help them see how exaggerated their reactions are and help them see how insignificant the situation is.

How to Treat Negative Self-Talk with NLP

Start paying attention to your inner critic. If you do have a few or many, just start with one. Pay attention to what the voice is saying. Consider it and decide if the voice is aggressive, loud, whispering, or shouting, and if it sounds like your own.

Reflect on your feelings as you hear the voice. Does it cause you to question? Does it enrage you? Does it cause you to feel down? Just take a moment to assess your emotional state.

Move the inner voice mentally to an extremity of your body, like your thumb or big toe. Does that alter the mood? Is the voice coming from across the room or right into your ear? Notice how the sound changes when you move the voice to a different body part.

The exciting part is about to begin. Add static, as you may hear via a broken TV cable or over the radio. Consider turning up the volume to silence the voice further using humorous music. Check-in with your feelings once more.

Try swapping the voice for "Porky Pig" or any other humorous voice-over or cartoon character you choose now. Play your favorite songs in funny tones as well. Note your current feelings.

Now start talking to your voice in your head, telling it to stop criticizing and reminding you of your shortcomings and why you might not be able to accomplish certain things. Instead, start talking to it about the wonderful possibilities ahead of you and what you do well.

The Benefits Of Priming As A Technique

This is why using priming in persuasion is beneficial:

Priming facilitates efficient communication: Using priming to convey your message is a good idea. You can easily accomplish your motive using words, thoughts, and concepts linked to your aim.

Priming enables you to covertly complete your task: You can utilize priming to your advantage if you have a hidden agenda. Priming is the go-to tactic, for example, if you want to influence someone without them realizing your underlying motivation. This argument is easily understood if you have seen the well-known film Focus with Will Smith.

Will Smith portrays Nicky, a conman, in the film. He intends to defraud renowned Chinese gambler Tse. He bets a lot of money and loses it to Tse; he then asks Tse to select any player he wants, on or off the pitch, to win it back. Nicky will get his entire investment returned if his companion Jess correctly guesses the number.

Jess finds the concept offensive, but Nicky persuades her to accept the risk. Taking the binoculars, she scanned the field and spotted Farhad, one of Nicky's friends, sporting a jersey with the number 55 on it. She chooses that number after realizing this is a red flag for a scam. Jess and Nicky prevail in the bet.

Nicky informs Jess that he primed Tse's head with the number by showing it throughout the day, and she later asks him how he pulled off that deception.

Nicky gets Tses to choose that specific number and wins millions of dollars by putting 55 in his head.

Priming enables you to address your audience's subconscious: Priming is an excellent strategy for invading your subconscious and taking control of it to achieve your objectives. You can force someone to follow your instructions or reach the desired conclusion by only putting something similar in their head.

As you can see, priming is a highly useful strategy for achieving your objectives. Here are some real-world instances of priming in action and practice exercises for this method.

Priming facilitates efficient product marketing: You may increase the sales on your website and effectively market your products by using priming. You only need to emphasize a product's main advantages and repeatedly prime it in your target audience's subconscious to pique their attention and draw them in.

Consider the Macy's website sales page for a weather-resistant jacket. Macy's goal with this specific item is to increase sales by emphasizing the jacket's best attribute: its ability to withstand weather. Macy's wishes its customers to think this jacket is the best weatherproof. They employ repeated priming to do this. The terms "windbreaker" and "weather resistant" are used several times in the product description on their website to highlight the jacket's salient features and instill these terms in the minds of potential customers. Buyers who intend to purchase a weather-resistant jacket retain these keywords and remember the item. You will start to see this tactic everywhere in marketing and promotional materials if you begin to pay attention to it!

You may easily persuade people when you prime them: Sarah would like her husband Jason to get her a pearl necklace for her birthday. She doesn't want to tell Jason directly, though. She devises a scheme to instill in Jason the notion of buying her a pearl necklace.

During their morning tea, Sarah shows Jason a photograph of a pearl necklace from a magazine she reads and expresses her admiration for it.

Sarah informs Jason later that evening, just before bed, that her best friend bought a pearl necklace from Zales and that she is saving money to get one for herself. Sarah brings up the pearl necklace again the following day, stating that she feels incomplete without it on her blue outfit. She primes Jason's subconscious with the "pearl necklace" in this fashion.

Three days later, while shopping for Sarah's birthday present, Jason thinks she would adore a pearl necklace and heads to the jewelry store to get one.

The instances above demonstrate how effective priming is at helping you discreetly convey your motivation.

Now that you know that, here is how to apply this method in practical situations.

How to Apply Priming

The priming approach can be applied to both yourself and other people in the following ways:

Using priming to persuade people

Give someone a clear goal to stimulate them. How would you like the person to respond? Why do you wish to convince the other person? Do you want the other person to support your decision, or do you want them to do an errand for you?

Determine the motivation behind your desire to convince someone, then record it in your journal.

Once you have a clear motive, find words, phrases, and sentences that fit the bill. For example, you could say, "I feel like drinking tea, or Ooh, how I wish I could drink a warm cup of tea, but I have to work on this project report right now," to your partner in place of asking her to make you a cup of tea. Create a few different suggestive phrases that you may use and keep them handy. Next, pick the most suitable one for the discussion when it comes up.

Next, speak to the individual you wish to influence informally and confidently using the selected words or phrases. While doing so, avoid dropping your gaze or breaking direct eye contact with the person, as these actions indicate being secretive, having a hidden agenda, and hiding something.

After a five-to-one-hour break, repeat the selected sentences or comparable sentences. The idea will eventually get ingrained in the person's memory. Track any indications that your suggestion has been implemented, and look for success stories.

N.L.P. Instructors

Both N.L.P. practitioners and N.L.P. Master practitioners are trained at this stage. It demonstrates the special fusion of learning how to be a presenter and a trainer. Furthermore, being aware of the distinction. They gain knowledge on how to become more self-assured, enjoy what they do, and interact with others in a relaxed manner.

They are expected to become charismatic, transformed presenters after the training. The methods and abilities kids pick up enable them to study, comprehend, and impact others in groups. When they finish their studies, they can coordinate with other groups, master a skill, and give a presentation to an audience while feeling more confident.

..

The N.L.P. Strategy: Internal and External

The primary focus of N.L.P. techniques is exposure, both external and internal. Every experience yields well-known results. Regardless of the order, a defined product is always achieved for both internal and external experiences. Getting the greatest results becomes challenging when the sequence and flow are altered. For example, to receive a response to an email you wrote, you must use all of your established internal and external communication experience. Additionally, all planned outcomes won't be successful if the technique is altered.

It always uses a variety of senses, including the gustatory, kinesthetic, aural, visual, and olfactory, to get into all the techniques. It's possible to initiate the outward habit of responding to emails, which might create an inside experience and a particular perception. As a result, some habits will develop. It's crucial to remember that the sensory experiences mentioned above can occur both inside and outwardly. For instance, an N.L.P. therapist will constantly discuss your internal and external experiences during the session. And what they do is make sure that the tactics that are employed are better understood.

The Model of T.O.T.E.

Brandler and Grinder, the creators of N.L.P., also discussed another paradigm called T.O.T.E. This model, which elaborates on how someone else will interpret information, employs many N.L.P. methodologies. T.O.T.E. stands for "Test, Operate, Test, and Exit." This tactic connects to a book by Miller, Pribram, and Galanter, although it largely relates to Bandler and Grinder.

One reacts because the model was used to measure the processes. It determines what primarily sets a habit apart from any strategy. It examines how the strategy is initiated and whether the process repeats itself when tested. For instance, encouraging oneself to compose emails or what first spurred you to pick up the pen. Subsequently, that serves as the trigger, initiating the test and ultimately determining whether or not to begin the writing technique.

The operation, which examines the internal and external procedures required for the strategy to begin and continue, is included in the model. An additional test is conducted to determine the trigger and the initiated process. Next, ascertain whether the habit and tactical approach in the first test were the same. When the exit strategy is effective, it will be revealed. If not, it's important to determine whether the experiences were the same or different from those in the second phase of the operation and whether the trigger was right.

Advantages of N.L.P. for Those Who Use It

A lot of N.L.P. has been eloquently illustrated in the preceding chapters. The various supporters within the system and how it affects various people's lives. Among them are:

• Assists in reducing tension and worry

This kind of natural therapy works well for other people who are experiencing anxiety, and N.L.P. provides similar relief. A study that was done demonstrates how N.L.P. has helped several claustrophobics. The anxiousness was reduced when M.R.I. scans were performed. It lessens tension and anxiety through the application of language mechanisms. When nervous, they can discuss the issue and feel at ease.

- It Enhances Commercial Achievement

N.L.P. has aided in changing behaviors to fit the objectives and goals of businesses and professional careers. It is beneficial without the individual considering how to be a slave to their work and not be productive. The bottom line is that forming new habits helps break bad ones, which leads to commercial success.

- Fosters Creativity

N.L.P. employs methods, tactics, and strategies that foster creativity in its practitioners when you know how several senses affect a person's conduct. After that, try out various tactics.

- Assists in Vanquishing Phobia and Fear

It concentrates on methods that comprehend tactics, safeguard and improve habits. This aids in altering the internal response and lessens fear and phobias.

• Enhances Relationships and Health

N.L.P. enhances relationships and overall health. It lowers the degree of depression and aids in enhancing coping mechanisms. In actuality, people can transform their vices into virtues. It aids in reducing anxiety, which always has a detrimental impact on one's life and well-being. This idea prioritizes and consistently strives to enhance our comprehension of human behavior. Interpersonal relationships are enhanced. There is an increased comprehension of the actions and behaviors of others.

What Does A Psychologist Understand By Psychopathy?

Psychopathy is a concept for the entirety of the personality property complex. Psychopathy is currently rarely used in psychiatry, as the term "dissociative (antisocial) personality disorder" has gained greater traction. In psychiatry, the psychiatrist treats mental illnesses rather than psychological disorders of personality and character. But a psychologist conducting a consultation may employ the terms psychopathy, impulsive psychopathy, and sociopathy—but only with moral caution. When a psychologist uses the terms psychopathy, impulsive psychopathy, and sociopathy, they are not referring to a mental illness but rather a marked degree of some psychological traits of the personality. Which attributes?

To put it simply, the impulsivity of the neurological system and psyche, aggressive tendencies in the psyche, a disdain for danger, and social norms of behavior all contribute to the development of psychopathy. It can appear to be bravery during a conflict. However, impulsive psychopathy frequently manifests itself in asocial ways during times of peace in human society. When someone turns into a sociopath, they can still be intelligent, rebellious, and compassionate at the same time. Conversely, this individual is intolerable and unable to deal with others.

Psychology defined a group of characteristics associated with sociopathy in the 1940s. The ability to make a good impression on first impressions (external charm), fearlessness, low anxiety, non-binding, dishonesty, insincerity, lack of regret and remorse, propensity for antisocial behavior, pathological egocentrism, and poverty of the emotional sphere were among the qualities that were specifically included.

And this is what they already wrote in 2006 on individuals who exhibit high degrees of impulsive psychopathy.

Psychologists Babiak and Hare: "People with psychopathy are not limited to prison environments; they can operate in a range of life scenarios." discussed, for instance, the prosperous professional lives of individuals with high levels of non-clinical psychopathy, despite the unpleasant nature of their workplace (colleagues refer to them as "snakes in suits").

Robert Hare wrote a lot of fascinating works overall. Take the "Control List of Signs of Psychopathy," for instance, which served as the foundation for a psychodiagnostic method used to identify psychopaths in the general public. And this amazing book, "Without Conscience," has a very poetic title.

In "Successful Brains," our private psychological program, we frequently encounter impulsive psychopathy in its expressions. For this reason, we have established our own subjective set of standards to characterize psychopathy. The following indicators can be used to identify impulsive psychopathy in a person under long-term observation:

The high degree of self-centeredness and willfulness (wanted to do!), lack of ability, indifference to the interests and feelings of others, and curiosity about other people's experiences. Impulsive psychopaths may appear like devoted villains in circumstances where they affect other people's interests, but in actuality, they simply don't give a damn about what happens to other people. They can aim for dominance and leadership without any reason by satisfying their unquenchable cravings.

Anger, irritation, or hate in any form:

Physical or verbal aggression.

Persistent defamation (speaking poorly of others).

Extremely sardonic humor (laughing at things you wouldn't laugh at).

Anger, mindless brutality (where deterrents are present—emotional). Concurrently, during "calm" moments, impulsive psychopaths might exhibit extraordinary politeness, a purposeful grin, and "epileptoid sweetness."

Aggressive conduct suddenly and suddenly changes in behavior.

Psychopaths of the impulsive cycloid type build-up neuro-mental stress, which they then release as conflict or hostility. This cycle is then perpetually repeated. The impulsive psychopath initiates conflict and aggressiveness when there isn't one. When visiting a psychologist, victims of impulsive psychopaths typically claim that the aggressor "took the occasion," "invented the occasion," or "provoked the conflict," and in many situations, this is accurate. It is necessary for the impulsive psychopath cycloid type to release his neuro-mental stress through conflict or hostility, after all. And he recognizes this necessity without considering the emotions or interests of others.

Irresponsibility and contempt for obligations, regulations, and social conventions. Lack of shame and a propensity to place blame elsewhere. The desire to live an inactive or asocial lifestyle, such as not working but instead choosing to pursue a fun pastime or stay out of his family's life. Instances of the impulsive psychopath's foolish and immature actions include "eternal teenager," "always a fighter," "real macho," and "fighter for justice." This can be a very alluring option for some close individuals, up until they have to deal with the consequences of impulsive psychopath conduct.

In close partnerships, there is a great reluctance to establish enduring friendships based on cooperation, compromise, and mutual understanding. Egocentrism, emotional indifference, and disregard for the needs and feelings of those close to you. Animosity or aggression toward those who are closest to you. Releasing tensions and upsetting feelings in relationships with close ones. Frequently dishonest and retaliatory. Typically, family members feel that this type of person is unnecessary and unimportant. It is, in theory. And this is a common criticism of a psychologist's counsel.

Unwillingness and incapacity to weigh the long-term harm that their actions would cause. In extreme situations, impulsive psychopaths can be more likely to commit acts of violence, sexual misbehavior, stealing, vagrancy, repeatedly lying, breaching the law, violating customs, and occasionally becoming intoxicated or addicted to drugs, among other antisocial behaviors.

Because they could be indifferent to consequences, threats to life, hardships, and deprivation, impulsive psychopaths can be harmful to both themselves and other people. In extreme situations, the only things that can contain an impulsive psychopath like him are physical constraints or terror. The problem with impulsivity is that an impulsive psychopath does not make sense of his experiences or form conclusions. However, in less severe situations, the advantage or diversion from physical or mental activity may prevent impulsive psychopaths from acting out.

It has all of the indicators above, though not always in conjunction with psychopathic traits in the individual's personality. There may be one or two, but they are expressed excessively—insufficiently, not fact, at their height. Like any diagnosis, though, the psychological diagnosis of psychopathy necessitates a thorough examination of the entire set of features as well as a broad examination of a wide range of personality attributes.

Naturally, a psychologist must use rigorous psychodiagnostic techniques in addition to observation to stage a psychological (not psychiatric!) diagnosis of psychopathy. Non-clinical psychopathy is harder to identify and diagnose than narcissism. A psychologist can utilize the Psychopath Personality Inventory (PPI) or its revised version, the Psychopath Personality Inventory-Revised (PPI-R), to diagnose psychopathy. Our publications "Psychologist's Consultation: Impulsive Psychopathy" and "Psychologist's Consultation: Sociopathicism" contain some information about psychopathy and sociopathy. The psychologist could suggest speaking with a psychiatrist to provide additional clarity in clinical instances.

Neuro-Linguistic Programming offers tools and strategies exclusive to this kind of learning. Recall that while it isn't therapy, its foundations are in therapeutic methods that help you understand the life you are living in the present, process your human experience by connecting it to family dynamics, and use advanced hypnotherapy techniques that reach deeper into the mind to reveal more of our unconscious behaviors. You can progress through four learning phases by using the tools in this toolbox in conjunction with practice until they become ingrained in your daily life. The way your mind functions when you learn anything new is like follows:

Firstly, you are incompetent without even realizing it, a condition known as unconscious incompetence. It is right before you, ready to be modeled, but you just don't know what you don't know.

The next stage is called incompetent consciousness, which denotes that although you are fully aware of the steps needed to complete a task or accomplish an objective, you are still learning the process and may feel uncomfortable during the learning curve.

When you are consciously competent, you understand and can apply what you have learned but still need to work on perfecting it.

At the end of the learning process, you become unconsciously competent when you can easily integrate your new talents with your general conscious awareness. This is performing a task, such as driving a car or brushing your teeth, in a certain way without understanding how skilled you are.

You will be learning, unlearning, and relearning mental and linguistic systems that can shape your experience as you move through the upcoming chapters. With time, the knowledge you acquire will contribute to your self-awareness regarding your responses, actions, and dispositions and enhance your ability to recognize these patterns in other people.

Making Use of Creative Visualization

Much of what you study in NLPinvolves using your imagination and creativity. As you have read in previous chapters, your mind uses your senses to experience, store, and retrieve memories. We often create internal images in "the mind's eye" without realizing it. You can see and feel the past again here, envision the future, and change how you view the world. NLPlets you interact with your senses and understand your brain's functions. We cannot precisely predict the future or reproduce or relive events that have already happened. The current moment is all that we are genuinely capable of perceiving.

That's how using creative visualization to practice NLPskills can be helpful. You frequently use your mental image to reframe and reintegrate past events differently. You will also be able to use a technique known as "Future Pacing," a term from NLPthat involves picturing yourself in a scenario to experience it beforehand with the assurance you desire. Future speed takes any form of issue, problem, challenge, or constraint and lets you perceive it as though it were happening in your head. When you utilize this strategy, you can combine the elements you want and delete the portions you don't. Parts are analogous to actions, attitudes, or unfavorable mental processes.

An illustration of what that looks like:

Let's imagine you have a big presentation at work coming up, and it may place you in line for that promotion you have been craving. The last time you gave a presentation, it didn't go how you had hoped because you felt nervous, unprepared, and worried that someone would give a more well-planned and confident work report. You can use the future pacing technique to prepare for this upcoming presentation. This technique is usually performed after you have integrated some other NLPtraining tools; however, this example outlines the concept of visualization and its impact on your mental process in a future event. So, before this presentation, create a mental rehearsal in your mind. When doing this, you must close your eyes to truly see the experience's image.

When you imagine yourself in the conference room, notice how it feels. Does your posture change? Do you begin to feel uncertain or insecure? If yes, you can utilize some visualization to help you reframe your potential experience. Remember a time in your life when you felt confident and secure. Remember a time in your life when you felt well-spoken and calm. Remember a time in your life when you felt a sense of achievement and accomplishment. Hold those feelings in your mind and your body.

Keeping your eyes closed, imagine yourself in this state of awareness while giving your presentation. Imagine a color that makes you feel all of those positive feelings. Imagine that while feeling those positive feelings, the bright color encircles you. You can also imagine a smell that you find uplifting, refreshing, and energizing. Bring in the smell of citrus-like orange and have that color bright all around you. As you are rehearsing your presentation in your imagination, anytime you feel less confident, anxious or flustered, see the color dimming and the scent dissipating. You will notice this change in your behavior more if the light dims and the orange is no longer the aroma of awareness.

When you have this sensory awareness of your experience changing, you know how to rekindle it. Turn the light brighter, and put a whole basket of oranges in the room. Cover the floor with oranges if you have to. When you draw awareness to your change in attitude and behavior, you can change it and using creative visualization as a tool to do this will be used throughout the NLPtechniques in this book. You can use creative visualization for anything; there is no right or wrong way. Remember, you have a unique brain, unlike anyone else's. The ideas you come up with when you visualize belong to your subjective experience and will always be most meaningful to you the way you see them.

It is an amazing way to connect to your creativity, another one of NLP's amazing benefits. When you use your mind to imagine, you can think way outside the box of patterns and behaviors you have been running in your mental programming for so long.

Link The Prospects Need to Your Product or Service
Step 4 could be a course all on its own. But I will give you the quick, actionable

tips that will help you the most. The basis of Step 4 is to link the need you established with Step 3 to your product or service.

In general, features are not useful to a prospect. They want to hear the benefits. You want to establish the "how" by giving as few details as possible. Let's go back to our car-buying prospect who wanted a safe vehicle. Here, I'll show you exactly why you want to tell a prospect as little as possible about how your product or service will solve their problem. So, the wrong way to link value would be:

"So Mr. Prospect, we have established that you need a car that is very safe. Well, car XYZ here has twelve dual-stage airbags, seatbelt pre-tensioners, adaptive cruise control, and blah blahblah."

Do you know what your prospect is going to say?

"Oh my, I heard that dual-stage airbags kill babies in car seats. I don't want to buy that car."

You immediately have an objection. The more details you give, the more objections you'll have to handle, and you haven't even tried to close yet!

The correct way to link value would be:

"Mr.prospect, we established that you need a safe car for you and your wife. I want to show you the XYZ coach. It has the highest safety ratings in the industry."

This car meets his needs and solves the prospect's need for a safe car. Is he going to object to a safe car? Probably not. You didn't give him much to object to. The car meets his needs. He may come up with an objection, but at least you didn't supply it. Don't give your prospect ammo to shoot you down.

In Step 4, you also want to introduce frames. Frames are incredibly easy and powerfully persuasive. Imagine you took a wonderful picture of a sunset, but in the bottom corner, there's some overweight guy in a Speedo. Do you let that one flaw ruin your whole picture? Of course not. You go into Photoshop and reframe this photo to exclude the overweight guy. Frames, just like the name implies, put a border around something. A frame is a way of focusing your prospect's attention on a certain area. Let's take a closer look at a few of these frames.

First off, there's the "What if..." frame. I love this frame. This frame allows you to let your prospect imagine away some self-imposed limitations. Say you have a prospect who tells you he is very interested in your product or service, but he has some hesitation. Go ahead and ask him:

"What would happen if you purchased this product or service today?"

Let him answer his question by imagining himself purchasing your product or service. Now that he has imagined purchasing your product or service closing him will be much easier. He has already imagined owning the product, so as long as you have established enough value, buying becomes a no-brainer at this point.

Another example of framing is to use the negative "What if...?"

"What if you don't solve this problem? Imagine how your life will be in 5, 10, 20 years with all of that pain you could have avoided."

Yet another frame is the Contrast. This frame allows you to compare your product or service to another with lesser quality. Instead of saying:

"This is the safest car available," you could say. "This model XYZ is rated five stars compared to (cheaper) model XYY, which is rated only two stars."

With the Comparison frame, you are limiting the prospect's available choices. This is a standard practice in real estate. You show the prospect a beat-up cheap house (fixer-upper). Then, you show the prospect a beautiful house that is out of his price range. Finally, you take the prospect to a nice house within the price range (the one you intended to sell them all along). By giving the prospect a contrast, you are helping them to decide to buy the best house they can afford.

Suddenly, the middle house is so nice compared to the fixer-upper and inexpensive compared to the big house. The middle house is just right. The prospect is happy with their purchase, and you helped them get into the right house. You have created a win/win situation.

Also, try contrasting life now (the boring, painful, dreary, whatever problem the prospect has) with the new life of excitement, fun, and adventure of having your product or service. I heard a travel agent use this one to great effect. He said:

"Considerate yourself and your friends sitting at the bar next month. Telling the same old stories gets boring. Imagine how jealous your friends will be.

That was the prospect's hot button, as shown by the fact that he purchased the cruise. Before you say anything, you must be certain of your prospect's internal definition of success for this hot-button strategy to be effective.

The Agreement frame is the final frame I want to discuss. This is not the approach where you ask your prospect questions in the hopes that he will say "yes" to them. The Agreement frame is considerably easier. This is a frame that I typically employ when addressing an objection, but it also functions nicely for Step 4. "I agree and..." or "I appreciate that, and..." are the essential components of the Agreement frame.

For instance, you might hear from your prospect, "I like the color." "I agree, anally meets your needs for safety" is one way you could respond. As for "I appreciate that, and it really meets your needs for safety." In that instance, you're making a connection between something they enjoy and the need they claim to have. This enhances the car's appeal and fulfills my needs, making it even better!

It's a terrific opportunity to apply strategies. Let's say a potential customer informs you that he typically does his homework on products, reading evaluations before looking at them in person. Take note of how you lead him through each step in the example below:

"Mr. Prospect, now that you've gotten all sorts of information from me about the car, read some of the customer reviews I showed you, and taken a good look at the car, you can definitely see that this is the car you want, can't you?" (As you nod your head).

You won't realize how effective this is until you see the prospect's eyes light up. That you made purchasing your good or service so simple for him will make him very happy. How come he wouldn't be? He needed a problem solved, and you helped him get it done!

As an additional illustration, what if you contacted me for private coaching? You wish to let go of a self-limiting idea that you hold. You solve your difficulty when I assist you in doing this. You're more inclined to refer me to others if I make the procedure as simple as possible for you. This also applies to you and your prospects. If they were unwilling to buy, they wouldn't correspond with you. You should have eliminated those for whom

your product or service is ineffective if
you've done your job well.

Nlp-Based Mind Control For Love And Relationships

One must first comprehend mind control independently to comprehend how it functions in tandem with NLP.

Mind Control: What Is It?
When someone or something is in charge of someone else's ideas and behavior, it is called mind control. This is achievable by using words and actions to access one's mind and make it do anything for you. One may wonder if it is even feasible to control someone's thoughts. Then, the response is in the affirmative—it is feasible. Though it is just a psychological approach rather than a physical one, one may mistakenly believe that entering the brain is the way to do it.

Hypnosis is a useful technique for accessing the unconscious mind; it is one approach. The majority of the mind is unconscious. The pre-conscious, located in the middle of the brain, and the conscious, the smallest section of the brain, are the other components. The unconscious taps into the majority of old memories. Since there are many unsolved questions, someone who taps into it can modify someone's current. When unanswered questions are addressed, more of the past is created, influencing the present.

In psychotherapy, but particularly in psychoanalysis, is the process of tapping into the unconscious. The type of therapy known as psychoanalysis was developed to address issues that are not present at the moment. Sigmund Freud developed psychoanalysis, which Erick Erickson subsequently revised. This type of treatment aimed to shed light on the past. This illustrates mind control in some way. What sense, one would wonder? That's only the impression that the so-called confusing past has been clarified in that others can awaken and use the brain in any way they see fit.

NLPis a communication type made possible by the brain, which interprets and transmits information through waves that are read. NLP was briefly discussed in the last chapter and effectively addresses issues related to the brain's neurology. This neural programming makes this larger-scale reading and understanding of the mind possible. So, how can mind control and NLP work together?

Discussing mind control with NLP is straightforward. It is clear how they cooperate. While mind control involves figuring out how to get the mind or brain to obey a command, NLP communication focuses on understanding the mind psychologically. Its name essentially implies that. So, how are they connected? When the mind is required to accept and process information, this is known as mind control. This is made feasible via NLP, a communication method that uses coded signals to transmit and receive information. These coded communications allow the mind to process and ultimately understand the message the body will eventually follow and respond to.

How Do NLPand Mind Control Affect Love and Relationships?

Everybody experiences relationships and love daily. Relationships and love can include friendships, family, marriage, and coworkers. Understanding social institutions is a prerequisite to understanding love and relationships. This entails comprehending the settings and dynamics of these romantic partnerships. One must set their mind to establishing love before pursuing a relationship.

There must be a connection for love to flourish. That denotes a steady setting where individuals get together and create unique bonds. For example, people who live close to one another build friendships. Another requirement for the relationship is that the individuals, or at least two of them, must share interests or common goals. Establishing common ground is essential for fostering a friendship. As a result, friendship turns into a family, and friends support and counsel you. Without friendship, one would be alone and, therefore, a loner. Friendship is a vital institution in life.

Marriage is an additional romantic and social bond. A marriage is a relationship between two people. It is said to be highly significant in someone's life. Friendships first lead to close relationships, which lead to marriage and a lifetime of togetherness. The statement above does not cover certain marriage relationships. Given that it comprises two people with disparate viewpoints and operation methods, marriage is simple and complex. It's acceptable for the spouses to dispute because of their differences, which keeps the marriage strong—unlike when couples share similar traits.

Beyond love, family is another kind of interaction. Families are formed via adoption, marriage, and blood relations. A family will always be there for you when no one else is, even though they can sometimes be unpleasant. They are always there to aid someone with anything. Physical, mental, emotional, and financial issues could be involved.

Family is a solid foundation in human existence. In a lot of ways, it comes first. It originates from someone's first language, etiquette, and, for some, their faith. It is the initial socialization that all children receive while growing up.

A person's place of employment is another social setting. Numerous people become connected to someone because of their place of employment. Even if work is formal, it nevertheless strengthens relationships. Some coworkers may find love, friendship, or even marriage due to their jobs. People who work feel more stable. Thus, coworkers support one another through the chaos of the workplace and become close friends because they operate in similar environments. Coworkers understand most aspects of a person's day, and friends are there to support you through difficult times. It's fantastic to hang out with other individuals at work.

In the case of love, mind control and NLPcomplement each other. Love and relationships originate in the mind. Then, the mindset needs to be for them to function successfully. People think that relationships and love can transform people. People grow closer to their friends and lovers and more open and sympathetic. Love endures, and some people think it renders one stupid—not in the sense of a book, but rather in terms of ideas and deeds. Love can impact day-to-day existence and make people feel anxious and sensitive. Psyche-controlling and NLPhave a constant effect on the psyche. The mind is altered by love in both its functioning and its contents.

Relationships and love are difficult yet manageable since they keep people on their toes. People become closer to one another through relationships. This might exist anywhere at any time. It is impossible to survive without occasionally relating to other people. Love and relationships will always have an impact on the mind. A person in love has an optimistic and joyful outlook on life. Thus, connections and love allow people to be happy. Love plays a vital role in everyone's life. Everything gets more alive and easier.

Several Instances Of Manipulation In Our Everyday Lives

Manipulation exists everywhere. It can seem like everyone is out to get the others since so many people in our daily lives are trying to control and persuade others to agree with them. There are certain circumstances in which manipulation might become more obvious, and after going over a few of them, you might begin to realize that you have dealt with, or are dealing with, some of the examples listed below:

Advantage of Home Court

A person attempting to control another person will always look to take the initiative. It might be simpler for them to ask their victim to a meeting or engage in other activities in a physical location where the manipulator can exert greater authority and control. The victim may not be familiar with these places, but the manipulator may decide to meet with them to talk about something in the house, office, or car—any place where they feel more in control and at ease.

Since the victim believes the manipulator to be amiable and welcoming, they typically consent to meet here. The victim won't know this is happening until it's too late, but it gives the manipulator the advantage they seek.

Letting You Talk First

A common tactic used by manipulators is to let their victims speak first. This can function in various ways. In the first place, the victim will depart, believing they were in control. Furthermore, although the victim may believe that the manipulator is yielding to them, in practice, the manipulator prefers to let the victim speak first to establish a baseline for the victim's state of mind, identify any vulnerabilities, and then take advantage of these throughout the process.

You will notice this quite a bit in terms of sales. The salesperson will pose a series of pointed and generic questions to their target. This enables them to determine the victim's baseline for thought and behavior. They can see a clear picture of your strengths and flaws from here. There will be a hidden motive behind this kind of questioning, and we might encounter it in different contexts in our lives, such as interpersonal relationships and the job.

Swapping Out the Details

The manipulator will alter certain facts discussed in the discussion if they can get away with it. They will mostly take this action if they believe altering the situation will make them appear more favorable. Numerous instances of this can be observed in our daily existence. They could use exaggeration or exhibit a one-sided prejudice towards the problems. Occasionally, the manipulator will purposefully omit information that would help the victim make the best choice. They might attempt to place the responsibility for their victimization on the victim; they might twist the facts; they might lie, and they might also concoct justifications.

Including a tonne of facts and statistics

A common tactic used by manipulators against their victims is the notion of intellectual bullying. When the manipulator believes they are the most knowledgeable in a given field, they act this way. By exploiting their victim with purported facts, figures, and other information, the manipulator can carry out this tactic—especially if the victim is unfamiliar with the subject matter.

This kind of approach is something we might observe in sales and finance scenarios. The professional will assume that they have expert influence over you in these situations, and they think this will allow them to force their agenda more easily on you. Some individuals enjoy using this kind of strategy purely for the sake of feeling smarter than other people.

overwhelmingly Red Tape and You

The manipulator will employ numerous red tape and procedures to subjugate their victims in such situations. This strategy is referred to as bureaucracy. This will involve numerous rules and regulations, procedures, documentation, committees, and other impediments implemented purely to make the victim's life more challenging. The manipulator could use this tactic to delay gathering facts and obtaining the truth, in addition to giving them the upper hand over their victim. It is a great approach to divert the victim's attention from the manipulator if they sense they are being watched too closely. It can also assist in concealing the manipulator's shortcomings and shortcomings.

Speaking Up to Display the Negative Feelings

Raising their voice to ensure the victim is aware that they are experiencing bad emotions is the manipulator's next possible move. This frequently occurs during a conversation to demonstrate an aggressive manipulation technique. The manipulator presumes that the victim will be more likely to yield and give in to their demands if they project their voice loudly or exhibit enough negative emotions.

To convey their message even more, the manipulator frequently works on their body language and uses a loud, aggressive voice. They will ensure their body language is active to maximize the effect of what they are saying. Examples include standing erect and making gestures that convey wrath, enthusiasm, and other emotions.

Unexpected Behaviour Done in a Negative Way

Some manipulators enjoy using surprises that are regarded as dangerous to throw their victims off balance and to give them the psychological upper hand. The manipulator has multiple options for accomplishing this. They might play lowball during a negotiation, or the manipulator might suddenly reveal they cannot follow through on their previous commitments.

The victim will typically receive the unexpectedly bad news without any prior notice. As a result, it is difficult for the victim to plan and attempt to block the move in the desired manner. Ultimately, the manipulator may request further compromises from their target to maintain their working relationship.

Reducing the Time Allowed for Decision-Making

Limiting the time the other person has to decide is one tactic a manipulator may find helpful. The manipulator wants to see the victim comply with their wishes even if they are unsure of the choice or do not have enough time to consider all of their options. This is why the victim feels under pressure to make decisions quickly.

Giving the victim little time to decide is a common sales and collective bargaining strategy. Here is where the manipulator will frequently exert pressure on the target to decide before the victim is prepared to do so. It is hoped that by applying pressure and control to the other person, they will eventually break and submit to the aggressor's demands.

Examining Your Vulnerabilities

Certain manipulators enjoy making negative comments, which they try to pass off as humor or sarcasm. They can use this to make their target feel less confident and inferior, but when the victim begins to take offense, the fun lets the manipulator appear better and save face. They may also give the victim a sense of inadequacy and insecurity in the process.

When I think of this one, several examples spring to me. The manipulator may make remarks on your items, background, qualifications, appearance, and that you arrived at the workplace a few minutes late and appeared out of breath. The manipulator enjoys highlighting your mistakes to establish their psychological dominance over the victim.

Quick Cure for Phobias

A phobia is an unreasonable dread that causes an individual to overreact and lose control over their reaction, such as fainting. Even those who suffer from phobias are aware that their fears are unfounded and absurd, yet they are unable to control how they will react when their phobia flares up.

Removing phobias by changing their submodalities alone is a challenging task since phobias are harmful limiting beliefs. We require a blend of anchor, distortion, and submodalities; in NLP, this method is known as the "Fast Phobia Cure."

Quick Cure for Phobias

1. Picture yourself in a movie theatre.

Step inside the theatre and select a cozy seat.

2. Separate twice.

Step into the projection room, visualizing yourself beyond your physical form. You can see the screen and the person watching it in the projection room. It makes you feel secure to be there.

3. Play the film in monochrome.

Play the black and white movie in the projection room. Observe the person sitting next to you as they watch the movie. Start the video and watch it to the point where you are safe after experiencing the phobia. In the very last scene of the film, pause it!

4. Enter the screen.

Enter the screen. Enter your mind to witness the film as if it were yours. Restore color to the film by swiftly rewinding it to the beginning when you are safe.

5. Go back to the projector room after clearing the screen.

6. At least seven times, repeat steps 4 and 5.

7. Examine.

Consider something that could set off the phobia. How does it make you feel?

NLPMeditation and Hypnosis

Many people associate hypnosis and trance with visions of people acting against their will, swinging watches, and covert control.

There are many fallacies about hypnosis and trance that are grounded in fear rather than truth, as you will discover if you pick up any serious book on the subject or enroll in any genuine hypnotherapy school. These are some hypnotic concepts that you might want to verify for yourself.

One can hypnotize anyone. Rapid thinkers typically do not respond well to the usual, slow-moving trance induction because they become disinterested after a while. They react more favorably to brief inductions that use recommendations and pattern disruptions. Since everyone experiences some level of trance daily, we may claim that anyone can become hypnotized. additionally by "trance." I refer to this as a "heightened focus of attention" only.

We could even argue that we exist in a state of trance. Our days usually consist of paying attention to the outer world and indulging in trance states such as daydreaming, pondering, and remembering. A trance is when you focus one or more of your senses inward. Your senses become inwardly focused, and you somewhat detach from the outside world if you worry, recall a phone number, or reflect on the past. All of your senses are focused inward during a deep trance, although you can still hear the hypnotist's speech or the sound of a fire alarm. It will feel, at worst, like you've just woken up from a deep sleep.

Most likely, the medieval witches and magicians were hypnotists. Most likely, enchantments and magical spells were trances that were heightened by panic and anxiety. The reality of hypnosis is very different in the present world, where science and television have banished the myths and legends of our forefathers, even though some people still have similar concerns and anxieties.

Witchcraft is still a very potent social motivator in several parts of the world.

Therefore, using trance with your client fully engaged is natural and moral.

When was the last time you experienced a trance today?

When was the last time you unintentionally placed someone else in a trance?

Self-Mastery

Possessing total and constructive control over oneself is the essence of self-mastery. Unpleasant ideas that undermine your achievement can be controlled, and you can prevent unpleasant emotions from rising. This self-control is beneficial in stopping the feelings and behaviors that undermine your achievement. It can also assist you in achieving your objectives and achieving personal fulfillment.

Inner tranquility is the result of self-mastery. However, achieving actual serenity requires a lot of self-control. Frequently, you may feel your mind and body oppose your desires. Maintaining self-discipline and overcoming negative habits and tendencies can be an ongoing, everyday effort. Some people, such as yogis or Buddhist monks, devote their entire lives to practicing self-discipline. You are undoubtedly too busy to dedicate your whole life to mastering yourself because of your family, friends, job, school, hobbies, housework, and everything else you have on your plate. Thus, you'll be in luck if you can use NLPto rapidly and effectively fool your mind into exercising restraint.

Training in self-mastery frequently makes use of NLP. The fundamental idea of self-mastery The tenet of NLPis that self-control belongs to you. You may thus take charge of your own life by mastering the processes that govern your thoughts and brain. You may overcome negative and trivial feelings, such as jealousy, jealousy, or inadequacy, and end your self-defeating thoughts. You can also practice self-control and refrain from forming bad habits that will be bad for your success and well-being. These behaviors can include excessive eating, sleeping in, or fearing public speaking that interferes with your ability to perform your work.

The notion that you can shape and affect other people's behavior is another foundational idea in NLPthat supports self-mastery. Individuals rarely arbitrarily treat you. You shape how people see and react to you, consciously or unconsciously. You may take charge of your relationships by altering the way you show up and interact with people. This may significantly impact your ability to maintain self-control and the course of your life. You can experience improved treatment in your relationships, at corporate functions, and during job interviews. Having healthy and constructive connections may make a great difference in your life, as individuals impact every aspect of it.

Utilise Your Innate Talent

There is no difference between you and any other person in the world. You have all you need to thrive because of your innate ability. However, you have blocked out or removed some abilities for whatever reason. You are not living up to your full potential and genuinely think you are incapable of doing some things. You unintentionally deny yourself some of your achievements by believing that "I am incapable of doing that."

Why do you believe it is impossible? Maybe you thought someone in your life told you that you couldn't because they were in a position of authority over you. Perhaps you gave it up after trying it once and finding it uncomfortable or intolerable. You may have never attempted something before, yet because it's unfamiliar, you resist trying. You are depriving yourself of innate and natural abilities within you, regardless of the reason behind your refusal to believe in some of them.

You already possess all you need to thrive and survive in this world. You haven't gone far enough inside yourself to acquire certain skills. Your strong conviction that you "can't" may unintentionally prevent you from using certain abilities. Accept the idea that you are capable of everything and everything you set your mind to, and ignore the notion that you are incapable of doing a task.

You can benefit greatly from visualizing yourself accomplishing big things. Consider a skill you feel you lack, but that you know, you'll need to improve your life. Imagine that this talent is something you are chasing, like a fast-moving rabbit or bunny. Considering that this bunny rabbit is genetically engineered for speed, you could believe it is impossible to catch. Imagine, however, that you suddenly gain momentum. Suddenly, you have the strength and speed to grab the rabbit. Taste the victory when you've made the last lunge and have the rabbit in your hands. Take pride in who you are. You are rewiring your brain to believe you can acquire a skill or aptitude even when you think it will elude you.

Recite to yourself success mantras on a daily or even hourly basis. "I am capable of doing this. I'll carry this out. I have strength. I have skills. I was meant to be successful. Tell yourself what you need to hear to boost your confidence. Through auditory affirmation, your mind is trained to believe in itself.

Additionally, practice clearing your mind of unfavorable ideas. Think of them as dirt; they limit you and clog your mind.

When they begin to depress you, picture yourself getting up on a broom and sweeping them aside.

We talked about controlling your inner critic earlier. This is particularly crucial while overcoming negative self-beliefs, fear, and self-doubt. In this case, your inner critic is your enemy. Under the guise of "caution," it tries to hold you down. Never follow this inner voice of criticism. It is blatantly incorrect. Rather than taking the voice seriously and paying attention to its warnings, picture it speaking in a ridiculous cartoon voice so you may laugh at it. All hints of "you can't," "you are not good enough," or "it's not possible" should be ignored and transformed into cartoon absurdity. A louder voice yelling, "I can!" and "I am great!" and "This is very possible!" should be used in place of this one.

The mark of a real master communicator is this.

As we close this chapter, I encourage you to take a moment to evaluate your communication approach. Try to be aware of your posture, actions, behavior, and, most crucially, eye contact when engaging with friends, family, coworkers, and others. Based on these hints, you can determine what you need to improve on the most. Make a concentrated effort to improve your eye contact abilities if communicating is the most difficult part.

Please remember that practice is the most crucial element. Therefore, do take the time to develop the habit of using your newly acquired knowledge as soon as possible. You're going to witness the fruits of your labors soon.

The Basics Of Nonverbal Communication

We will look closely at body language in this chapter and show you how to use it immediately. The most crucial thing to remember from this chapter is to pay attention to positive and bad behaviors to establish a balanced approach to how you behave while evaluating other people.

As mentioned in the previous chapter, one of the most crucial areas you may concentrate on to enhance your communication abilities in general is body language. This implies that you can convey far more through your nonverbal cues—such as your posture, gestures, and facial expressions—than you may have intended to convey with your spoken words.

Your posture is arguably the most crucial aspect of body language you can focus on. Almost nobody pays any attention to this. Until someone points it out, you don't notice how you're standing. You may hear someone comment on how much you slouch or how much you are bent over when you sit.

Additionally, if sitting too much causes pain in your shoulders, back, or neck, you may start to pay attention to your posture. You can be stuck in unhealthy sitting and standing patterns when you start paying attention to your posture.

Taller people typically have trouble with posture since it might be difficult to maintain good posture. However, one of the things you should always be aware of when it comes to communication skills is appropriate posture.

Let's see an illustration of how posture is important for communicating.

At some point during a job interview, you will spend 99.99% of your time seated. Most instructors will now instruct you to sit straight and rest your hands on the edge of the desk or table. You violate the interviewer's personal space if you put your hands too close to their desk. Placing your palm on a table could be interpreted as an anxious position. You could appear extremely uptight or even nervous if you are excessively rigid. Slouching too much could be interpreted as disrespectful or indifferent.

Where is the balance, then?

Sitting like a regular person will help you maintain equilibrium. It's just a matter of manners; if you keep your elbows off the table and move your hands a little during the discussion, you'll come off as much more at ease and composed than if you're attempting to appear "perfect."

This example's underlying lesson is to be authentic. Humans have a stance that naturally exudes confidence, trust, and respect. You will appear excessively stiff if you adopt an overly erect stance. You may be completely ignored if you allow your shoulders to sag excessively.

But don't be alarmed. Practice is all you need to do if something is too difficult.

Putting your lower back into the back of your chair is a smart general rule of thumb. In this manner, the top of the chair's back and your upper back should be slightly apart. By doing this, you'll guarantee good posture. Just keep in mind to occasionally take a brief stroll around. This will make you appear carefree and at ease. If not, adopting a robotic demeanor can backfire.

How does this relate to individuals who read?

Take a moment to consider that.

Shoulder drooping is nearly always an obvious sign of an uneasy or defensive stance. The person may be only anxious or shy. You are approaching someone who is in a defensive posture in either scenario.

Crossed arms and knees are another obvious indicator of defensive posture. These are natural postures meant to shield the soft tissue beneath the rib cage, primarily the groin and abdominal regions. When someone is in one of these stances, you can guarantee they are either concealing something or defending themselves against an imagined danger.

Even though you may not have indicated any potential risks to this person, their placement reveals their feelings and thoughts. You are in a good position to obtain the advantage over that person if that is your goal.

However, please remember to keep your head and shoulders squared if you feel threatened or vulnerable (for whatever reason). This will indicate to your opponent that, despite your discomfort, you are stubborn.

www.ingramcontent.com/pod-product-compliance
Lightning Source LLC
Chambersburg PA
CBHW05215210526
44591CB00012B/1948